P9-CME-070

What GOD wants for Christmas™

Amy L. Gordon

Illustrations by
Lyuba Bogan

FAMILYLIFE™
Publishing

Little Rock, Arkansas

What God wants for Christmas? It's—to you—a surprise.

In box number seven it is disguised.

But—no peeking! Be patient! For this you must wait.

It's what you offer Him, and it's really great!

Gabriel

Luke 1:26

In the beginning, God started to plan
    To bring about Christmas,
            and it would be grand!
Here He would launch a gift-giving tradition.
    I'll tell how it started, so please pay attention.

But before we get to this story's heart
    Let me explain how I play a part.
I was involved, a long time ago,
    As angel and speaker; it's God's words I know.

For I stand in His presence. I'm Gabriel,
    And God wants you to hear the story I tell.
For my words will offer His great gift to you,
    And you'll know what He wants when the story
        is through.

What God wants for Christmas? It's—to you—a surprise.
    In box number seven it is disguised.
But—no peeking! Be patient! For this you must wait.
    It's what you offer Him, and it's really great!

Mary

Isaiah 7:14; Luke 1:26-38

This story began when Isaiah did tell
    That a virgin would give birth to Immanuel.
That name is special; it means "God with us."
    And one day in this Child, many would trust.

So when the time came, I was appointed
    To tell the young woman that she was anointed.
I said to her, "Mary, you're God's chosen one,
    And you will give birth to God's only Son."

"How can this be? For this isn't typical."
    "Indeed, it's not! We'll call it a miracle.
God's Holy Spirit will help you give birth
    To God-in-the-flesh. He'll live here on earth.

"God says to name this baby boy Jesus."
    Mary said, "Yes! May God do as He pleases.
For I am His servant, and I will obey
    So God can use me in this special way."

What God wants for Christmas? It's—to you—a surprise.
    In box number seven it is disguised.
But—no peeking! Be patient! For this you must wait.
    It's what you offer Him, and it's really great!

Joseph

Matthew 1:18-25

Sweet Mary now knew she'd be Jesus's mother,

    But moms need some help! She needed another.

And Jesus would soon need a here-on-earth dad.

    God knew all that! Here's the plan that He had:

God had a man named Joseph in mind;

    He'd make a good husband, who's loving and kind.

So one night God sent an angel to speak

    Instructions to Joseph while he lay asleep.

"Joseph! Take Mary. She'll be a good wife.

    This marriage is still God's plan for your life.

God's Spirit has given her a baby within;

    His name will be Jesus; He'll save you from sin."

What God wants for Christmas? It's—to you—a surprise.

    In box number seven it is disguised.

But—no peeking! Be patient! For this you must wait.

    It's what you offer Him, and it's really great!

Baby Jesus

Luke 2:1-7

After a while there came a decree:

    "Go back where you're from originally!"

So this couple set out to Bethlehem-town,

    And when they arrived, they looked all around.

But the inns were too full—no room for two guests,

    And Mary was tired; she needed to rest.

"All rooms are taken," the innkeeper said.

    But then an idea popped in his head.

"My stable's not much, but there you can stay.

    I'll give you this manger—a feed trough with hay."

Later on ... there ... in the quiet of night ...

    To Joseph and Mary's excited delight

She gave birth to God's Son. It was not a surprise.

    God said it would happen, and He never lies.

God gave the first gift that first Christmas Day.
  He gave us the Christ, the babe in the hay.
But that is not all—God wants something grand:
  An offering to Him, the point of His plan.

What God wants for Christmas? It's—to you—a surprise.
  In box number seven it is disguised.
But—no peeking! Be patient! For this you must wait.
  It's what you offer Him, and it's really great!

Shepherd

Luke 2:8-20

During the night, when all was quite still,
    Shepherds were sheep-watching out on a hill.
"A Savior is born!" boomed a rushing-wind voice.
    "I herald Messiah! It's time to rejoice!"

Now what stood before them? The angel in white—
    With eyes full of fire and stature of might.
"Go to Bethlehem, now; in a stable you'll find
    A babe in a manger—that is your sign."

Then finding a stable where they saw a light
    Shine through the wallboards and into the night,
The shepherds looked in, and what did they see?
    The manger! A baby! They fell to their knees.

"So this must be Him! This is the sign!"
    They had found Jesus—the Savior divine!
These shepherds joined in the first celebration
    Of Christmas because of this grand revelation.

What God wants for Christmas? It's—to you—a surprise.
    In box number seven it is disguised.
But—no peeking! Be patient! For this you must wait.
    It's what you offer Him, and it's really great!

Wise Man

Matthew 2:1-12; Luke 2:19

Now way in the East lived some men who were wise.
  They saw a new star when they looked to the skies.
"This must be the star written here in our book.
  It tells of a king ... Let's go take a look."

So they followed this star till it finally rested
  Where Mary, the mother, and Jesus were nested.
When they stepped inside, they all fell to the floor
  To worship the King—but then there was more!

These men gave Him frankincense, myrrh, and fine gold
  To honor the One the new star had foretold.
Then, in a dream, they learned not to go back
  By way of King Herod. He planned to attack!

So they chose to go home a different way;
  The Child's location they did not betray.
As Mary thought through these events in her mind,
  She said, "God is so loving, protective, and kind."

What God wants for Christmas? It's—to you—a surprise.
  In box number seven it is disguised.
But—no peeking! Be patient! For this you must wait.
  It's what you offer Him, and it's really great!

What God Wants

John 3:16; Romans 12:1

What God wants for Christmas? Now here's the surprise
    In box number seven, where it's been disguised.
Peek in the box, for so long you have waited.
    What God wants is you—the one He created!

"Me?" you ask. "Why is this so?"
    "I cannot wrap me and put on a bow!"
No, you cannot; but what you can give
    Are the choices you make in the life that you live.

God wants you to know Him and love Him within,
    And this is called worship, an offering to Him.
To do this, trust Jesus, who died in your place
    When you didn't deserve Him—that is called grace.

Pray now and offer your life and your heart.
    Say, "Jesus, I need You. I'd like a new start.
Forgive me today for the sins I've committed
    So one day in heaven I will be permitted."

When you pray this decision, the heavens rejoice
    That you have made worship of God your life's choice.
God wants you to know Him, so choose every day,
    To love God and thank God and give Him all praise!

Giving God What He Wants

The Bible tells us that God is love (1 John 4:8, 16), and that He adopts those who receive Jesus as God's own Son, believing in Jesus's name. Unfortunately, we all do things that are wrong. God has a rule that our wrongs or "sin" must be punished. Having sin in our lives makes it impossible for God to adopt us—unless our sin is somehow removed.

God made this possible through Jesus, His Son. Jesus was born about 2,000 years ago. He grew up without ever sinning—always trusting God, always doing what He said. Because He obeyed God perfectly, the Bible tells us that Jesus was and is the only One who could take the punishment for our sin (2 Corinthians 5:21). He did this by dying on a cross. After three days, He came back to life, showing His power over sin and death (1 Corinthians 15:3-4). Jesus gave His life as a gift to us so that our sin could be removed and we could be adopted into God's family.

There are some great things about being adopted by God. We can still keep our families on earth. God forgives us of our sin, which means the wrong things we've done and sometimes continue to do won't get us kicked out of God's family (1 John 1:9). God sends us His Spirit, who guides us as we make choices and helps us in our lives (Romans 8:16, Galatians 5:22-23). And best of all, when our physical body dies, our invisible part (our spirit) goes to heaven to live with God—forever! (See John 3:16, 14:1-4.)

If we want God to adopt us, we need for our sin to be removed. We do this by, first, telling God that we've done things that are wrong. We admit the worst sin from our past: not accepting Jesus as the only One who can remove our sin and not believing in His name. We thank Him for allowing Jesus to take our punishment for us. Next, we ask God to forgive us of our sin. And then we invite God's Spirit to guide us for the rest of our lives and help us keep from sinning. When we sin again, we ask God to forgive us. We trust that He will and recommit to following His guidance (Mark 1:14-15; 1 Corinthians 15:1-4).

If you want to be adopted into God's family, you might pray something like this:

Dear God, I know that I've done things that are wrong. I'm sorry; I want to change. Thank you for Jesus, Your unique and beloved Son. I believe in His name, that You sent Him to die in my place, and that You have forgiven me of my sin. Thank you for adopting me as your child. —Amen.

If you prayed and asked God to adopt you, the angels in heaven are now celebrating! God delights in adding you to His family (Luke 15:10)! Be sure to tell your family and your church family, too. Ask them to help you learn how to live your life trusting in God and in Jesus's name.